Open Court Reading

The Stand

A Division of The McGraw-Hill Companies

Columbus, Ohio

SRA/McGraw-Hill

*A Division of The **McGraw·Hill** Companies*

Send all inquiries to:
SRA/McGraw-Hill
250 Old Wilson Bridge Road
Suite 310
Worthington, OH 43085

ISBN 0-02-660866-9
 2 3 4 5 6 7 8 9 ML 04 03 02 01 00 99

Tess has a help stand!
No problem is too big.
No problem is too small.

T. Rex wants a snack.
"No problem!" says Tess.
"Yum, this should fill you up."

4

Greg's neck is stiff.
"No problem!" says Tess.
"A scarf of yarn will do the trick."

Carl has no pocket.
"No problem!" says Tess.
"This belt should fit you."

Deb can't paddle in the pond.
"No problem!" says Tess.
"You can rent a raft."

Tess has to rest.
"No problem!" yawns Tess.
"No problem in my yard at all!"